To Everett - Hope you enjoy the
Hoosier poet that Aunt Pat loved!
You were very special to her!

RILEY FARM-RHYMES

WITH COUNTRY PICTURES

Books By
James Whitcomb Riley

NEIGHBORLY POEMS

SKETCHES IN PROSE WITH INTERLUDING VERSES

AFTERWHILES

PIPES O' PAN AT ZEKESBURY (Prose and Verse)

RHYMES OF CHILDHOOD

THE FLYING ISLANDS OF THE NIGHT

GREEN FIELDS AND RUNNING BROOKS

ARMAZINDY

A CHILD-WORLD

HOME-FOLKS

HIS PA'S ROMANCE (Portrait by Clay)

————

GREENFIELD EDITION

Sold only in sets. Eleven volumes uniformly bound in sage-green
cloth, gilt top $13.50
The same in half-calf 27.00

————

OLD-FASHIONED ROSES (English Edition)

THE GOLDEN YEAR (English Edition)

POEMS HERE AT HOME

RUBÁIYÁT OF DOC SIFERS

THE BOOK OF JOYOUS CHILDREN

RILEY CHILD-RHYMES (Pictures by Vawter)

RILEY LOVE-LYRICS (Pictures by Dyer)

RILEY FARM-RHYMES (Pictures by Vawter)

RILEY SONGS O' CHEER (Pictures by Vawter)

AN OLD SWEETHEART OF MINE (Pictures by Christy)

OUT TO OLD AUNT MARY'S (Pictures by Christy)

A DEFECTIVE SANTA CLAUS (Forty Pictures by Relyea and Vawter)

As he leaves the house, bare-headed, and goes out to feed the stock

RILEY

FARM-RHYMES

JAMES WHITCOMB RILEY

WITH

COUNTRY PICTURES

BY

WILL VAWTER

INDIANA UNIVERSITY PRESS
BLOOMINGTON & INDIANAPOLIS

This book is a publication of

INDIANA UNIVERSITY PRESS
601 North Morton Street
Bloomington, Indiana 47404-3797 USA

www.iupress.indiana.edu

Telephone orders   800-842-6796
Fax orders   812-855-7931

Manufactured by Sheridan Books, Inc.,
Ann Arbor, Michigan (USA); March 2013

Cataloging information is available from the Library of Congress.

ISBN 978-0-253-00951-7 (cloth); 978-0-253-00959-3 (e-book)

1   2   3   4   5   18   17   16   15   14   13

THE deadnin' and the thicket's jes' a b'ilin' full o' June,
From the rattle o' the cricket, to the yaller-hammer's tune;
And the catbird in the bottom and sap-suck on the
    snag,
Seems 's ef they cain't—od-rot-'em!—jes' do nothin' else
    but brag!

There' music in the twitter o' the bluebird and the jay,
And that sassy little critter jes' a-pecking' all the day;
There' music in the "flicker," and there' music in the thrush,
And there' music in the snicker o' the chipmunk in the
    brush!—

There' music all around me!—And I go back—in a dream
Sweeter yit than ever found me fast asleep:—And, in the
    stream
That used to split the medder wher' the dandylions growed,
I stand knee-deep, and redder than the sunset down the
    road.

CONTENTS

ILLUSTRATIONS

xvii

ILLUSTRATIONS — *Continued*

RILEY FARM-RHYMES

THE ORCHARD LANDS OF LONG AGO

THE orchard lands of Long Ago!
O drowsy winds, awake, and blow
The snowy blossoms back to me,
And all the buds that used to be!
Blow back along the grassy ways
Of truant feet, and lift the haze
Of happy summer from the trees
That trail their tresses in the seas
Of grain that float and overflow
The orchard lands of Long Ago!

Blow back the melody that slips
In lazy laughter from the lips
That marvel much if any kiss
Is sweeter than the apple's is.
Blow back the twitter of the birds—
The lisp, the titter, and the words
Of merriment that found the shine
Of summer-time a glorious wine
That drenched the leaves that loved it so,
In orchard lands of Long Ago!

O memory! alight and sing
Where rosy-bellied pippins cling,
And golden russets glint and gleam,
As, in the old Arabian dream,
The fruits of that enchanted tree
The glad Aladdin robbed for me!
And, drowsy winds, awake and fan
My blood as when it overran
A heart ripe as the apples grow
In orchard lands of Long Ago!

WHEN THE FROST IS ON THE PUNKIN

WHEN the frost is on the punkin and the fodder's in
the shock,
And you hear the kyouck and gobble of the struttin'
turkey-cock,
And the clackin' of the guineys, and the cluckin' of the
hens,
And the rooster's hallylooyer as he tiptoes on the fence;
O, it's then's the times a feller is a-feelin' at his best,
With the risin' sun to greet him from a night of peaceful
rest,
As he leaves the house, bare-headed, and goes out to feed
the stock,
When the frost is on the punkin and the fodder's in the
shock.

They's something kindo' harty-like about the atmusfere
When the heat of summer's over and the coolin' fall is
    here—
Of course we miss the flowers, and the blossums on the
    trees,
And the mumble of the hummin'-birds and buzzin' of the
    bees;
But the air's so appetizin'; and the landscape through the
    haze
Of a crisp and sunny morning of the airly autumn days
Is a pictur' that no painter has the colorin' to mock—
When the frost is on the punkin and the fodder's in the
    shock.

The husky, rusty russel of the tossels of the corn,
And the raspin' of the tangled leaves, as golden as the
    morn;
The stubble in the furries—kindo' lonesome-like, but still
A-preachin' sermuns to us of the barns they growed to fill;
The strawstack in the medder, and the reaper in the shed;
The hosses in theyr stalls below—the clover overhead!—
O, it sets my hart a-clickin' like the tickin' of a clock,
When the frost is on the punkin and the fodder's in the
    shock!

Then your apples all is getherd, and the ones a feller keeps
Is poured around the celler-floor in red and yeller heaps;
And your cider-makin' 's over, and your wimmern-folks
     is through
With their mince and apple-butter, and theyr souse
     and saussage, too! . . .
I don't know how to tell it—but ef sich a thing could be
As the Angels wantin' boardin,' and they'd call around
     on *me*—
I'd want to 'commodate 'em—all the whole-indurin'
     flock—
When the frost is on the punkin and the fodder's in the
     shock!

WHEN THE GREEN GITS BACK IN THE TREES

IN Spring, when the green gits back in the trees,
    And the sun comes out and *stays,*
And yer boots pulls on with a good tight squeeze,
    And you think of yer bare-foot days;
When you *ort* to work and you want to *not,*
    And you and yer wife agrees
It's time to spade up the garden-lot,
    When the green gits back in the trees
        Well! work is the least o' *my* idees
        When the green, you know, gits back in the trees!

When the green gits back in the trees, and bees
    Is a-buzzin' aroun' ag'in
In that kind of a lazy go-as-you-please
    Old gait they bum roun' in;
When the groun's all bald whare the hay-rick stood,
    And the crick's riz, and the breeze
Coaxes the bloom in the old dogwood,
    And the green gits back in the trees,—
        I like, as I say, in sich scenes as these,
        The time when the green gits back in the trees!

When the whole tail-feathers o' Wintertime
    Is all pulled out and gone!
And the sap it thaws and begins to climb,
    And the swet it starts out on
A feller's forred, a-gittin' down
    At the old spring on his knees—
I kindo' like jest a-loaferin' roun'
    When the green gits back in the trees—
        Jest a-potterin' roun' as I—durn—please—
        When the green, you know, gits back in the trees!

WET-WEATHER TALK

IT hain't no use to grumble and complane;
  It's jest as cheap and easy to rejoice.—
When God sorts out the weather and sends rain
      W'y, rain's my choice.

Men ginerly, to all intents—
  Although they're apt to grumble some—
Puts most theyr trust in Providence,
  And takes things as they come—
    That is, the commonality
    Of men that's lived as long as me
    Has watched the world enugh to learn
    They're not the boss of this concern.

With *some,* of course, it's different—
   I've saw *young* men that knowed it all,
And didn't like the way things went
     On this terrestchul ball;—
        But all the same, the rain, some way,
        Rained jest as hard on picnic day;
        Er, when they railly *wanted* it,
        It mayby wouldn't rain a bit!

In this existunce, dry and wet
   Will overtake the best of men—
Some little skift o' clouds'll shet
     The sun off now and then.—
        And mayby, whilse you're wundern who
        You've fool-like lent your umbrell' to,
        And *want* it—out'll pop the sun,
        And you'll be glad you hain't got none!

It aggervates the farmers, too—
   They's too much wet, er too much sun,
Er work, er waitin' round to do
     Before the plowin' 's done:
        And mayby, like as not, the wheat,
        Jest as it's lookin' hard to beat,

Will ketch the storm—and jest about
The time the corn's a-jintin' out.

These-here *cy-clones* a-foolin' round—
    And back'ard crops!—and wind and rain!—
And yit the corn that's wallerd down
    May elbow up again!—
        They hain't no sense, as I can see,
        Fer mortuls, sich as us, to be
        A-faultin' Natchur's wise intents,
        And lockin' horns with Providence!

It hain't no use to grumble and complane;
    It's jest as cheap and easy to rejoice.—
When God sorts out the weather and sends rain,
    W'y, rain's my choice.

THE BROOK-SONG

LITTLE brook! Little brook!
  You have such a happy look—
Such a very merry manner, as you swerve and curve
  and crook—
   And your ripples, one and one,
   Reach each other's hands and run
    Like laughing little children in the sun!

Little brook, sing to me:
Sing about a bumblebee
That tumbled from a lily-bell and grumbled mum-
blingly,
Because he wet the film
Of his wings, and had to swim,
While the water-bugs raced round and
laughed at him!

Little brook—sing a song
Of a leaf that sailed along
Down the golden-braided centre of your current
swift and strong,
And a dragon-fly that lit
On the tilting rim of it,
And rode away and wasn't scared a bit.

And sing—how oft in glee
Came a truant boy like me,
Who loved to lean and listen to your lilting melody,
Till the gurgle and refrain
Of your music in his brain
Wrought a happiness as keen to him as
pain.

Little brook—laugh and leap!
Do not let the dreamer weep;
Sing him all the songs of summer till he sink in
softest sleep;
And then sing soft and low
Through his dreams of long ago—
Sing back to him the rest he used to know!

THOUGHTS FER THE DISCURAGED
FARMER

THE summer winds is sniffin' round the bloomin'
      locus' trees;
And the clover in the pastur is a big day fer the bees,
And they been a-swiggin' honey, above board and on the
      sly,
Tel they stutter in theyr buzzin' and stagger as they fly.
The flicker on the fence-rail 'pears to jest spit on his wings
And roll up his feathers, by the sassy way he sings;
And the hoss-fly is a-whettin'-up his forelegs fer biz,
And the off-mare is a-switchin' all of her tale they is.

24

You can hear the blackbirds jawin' as they foller up the
      plow—
Oh, theyr bound to git theyr brekfast, and theyr not
      a-carin' how;
So they quarrel in the furries, and they quarrel on the
      wing—
But theyr peaceabler in pot-pies than any other thing:
And it's when I git my shotgun drawed up in stiddy rest,
She's as full of tribbelation as a yeller-jacket's nest;
And a few shots before dinner, when the sun's a-shinin'
      right,
Seems to kindo'-sorto' sharpen up a feller's appetite!

They's been a heap o' rain, but the sun's out to-day,
And the clouds of the wet spell is all cleared away,
And the woods is all the greener, and the grass is greener
      still;
It may rain again to-morry, but I don't think it will.
Some says the crops is ruined, and the corn's drownded
      out,
And propha-sy the wheat will be a failure, without doubt;
But the kind Providence that has never failed us yet,
Will be on hands onc't more at the 'leventh hour, I bet!

Does the medder-lark complane, as he swims high and dry
Through the waves of the wind and the blue of the sky?
Does the quail set up and whissel in a disappinted way,
Er hang his head in silunce, and sorrow all the day?
Is the chipmuck's health a-failin'?—Does he walk, er does
       he run?
Don't the buzzards ooze around up thare jest like they've
       allus done?
Is they anything the matter with the rooster's lungs er
       voice?
Ort a mortul be complanin' when dumb animals rejoice?

Then let us, one and all, be contentud with our lot;
The June is here this morning, and the sun is shining hot.
Oh! let us fill our harts up with the glory of the day,
And banish ev'ry doubt and care and sorrow fur away!
Whatever be our station, with Providence fer guide,
Sich fine circumstances ort to make us satisfied;
Fer the world is full of roses, and the roses full of dew,
And the dew is full of heavenly love that drips fer me
       and you.

"MYLO JONES'S WIFE"

M YLO Jones's wife" was all
    I heerd, mighty near, last Fall—
Visitun relations down
T'other side of Morgantown!
Mylo Jones's wife she does
This and that, and "those" and "thus"!—
Can't 'bide babies in her sight—
Ner no childern, day and night,
Whoopin' round the premises—
Ner no nothin' else, I guess!

Mylo Jones's wife she 'lows
She's the boss of her own house!—
Mylo—consequences is—
Stays whare things seem *some* like *his,*—
Uses, mostly, with the stock—
Coaxin' "Old Kate" not to balk,
Ner kick hoss-flies' branes out, ner
Act, I s'pose, so much like *her!*
Yit the wimmern-folks tells you
She's *perfection.*—Yes they do!

Mylo's wife she says she's found
Home hain't home with *men-folks* round
When they's work like *hern* to do-
Picklin' pears and *butchern,* too,
And a-rendern lard, and then
Cookin' fer a pack of men
To come trackin' up the flore
She's scrubbed *tel* she'll scrub no *more!*—
Yit she'd keep things clean ef they
Made her scrub tel Jedgmunt Day!

Mylo Jones's wife she sews
Carpet-rags and patches clothes

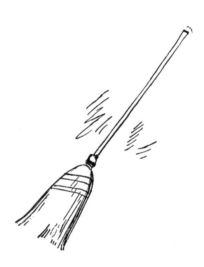

Jest year *in* and *out!*—and yit
Whare's the livin' use of it?
She asts Mylo that.—And he
Gits back whare he'd ruther be,
With his team;—jest *plows*—and don't
Never sware—like some folks won't!
Think ef *he'd cut loose,* I gum!
'D he'p his heavenly chances some!

Mylo's wife don't see no use,
Ner no reason ner excuse
Fer his pore relations to
Hang round like they allus do!
Thare 'bout onc't a year—and *she*—
She jest *ga'nts* 'em, folks tells me,
On spiced pears!—Pass Mylo one,
He says "No, he don't chuse none!"
Workin'men like Mylo they
'D ort to have *meat* ev'ry day!

Dad-burn Mylo Jones's wife!
Ruther rake a blame caseknife
'Crost my wizzen than to see
Sich a womern rulin' *me!*—

Ruther take and turn in and
Raise a fool mule-colt by hand!
Mylo, though—od-rot the man!—
Jest keeps ca'm—like some folks *can*—
And 'lows sich as her, I s'pose,
Is *Man's he'pmeet!*—Mercy knows!

HOW JOHN QUIT THE FARM

NOBODY on the old farm here but Mother, me and
      John,
Except, of course, the extry he'p when harvest-time
      comes on—
And *then,* I want to say to you, we *needed* he'p about,
As you'd admit, ef you'd a-seen the way the crops turned
      out!

A better quarter-section ner a richer soil warn't found
Than this-here old-home place o' ourn fer fifty miles
      around!—
The house was small—but plenty-big we found it from
      the day
That John—our only livin' son—packed up and went
      away.

You see, we tuk sich pride in John—his mother more'n
      me—
That's natchurul; but *both* of us was proud as proud
      could be;
Fer the boy, from a little chap, was most oncommon
      bright,
And seemed in work as well as play to take the same
      delight.

He allus went a-whistlin' round the place, as glad at
      heart
As robins up at five o'clock to git an airly start;
And many a time 'fore daylight Mother's waked me up
      to say—
"Jest listen, David!—listen!—Johnny's beat the birds
      to-day!"

High-sperited from boyhood, with a most inquirin' turn,—
He wanted to learn ever'thing on earth they was to learn:
He'd ast more plaguy questions in a mortal-minute here
Than his grandpap in Paradise could answer in a year!

And *read!* w'y, his own mother learnt him how to read
      and spell;
And "The Childern of the Abbey"—w'y, he knowed that
      book as well
At fifteen as his parents!—and "The Pilgrim's Progress,"
      too—
Jest knuckled down, the shaver did, and read 'em through
      and through!

At eighteen, Mother 'lowed the boy must have a better
      chance—
That we ort to educate him, under any circumstance;
And John he j'ined his mother, and they ding-donged and
      kep' on,
Tel I sent him off to school in town, half glad that he was
      gone.

But—I missed him—w'y, of course I did!—The Fall and
      Winter through
I never built the kitchen-fire, er split a stick in two,

Er fed the stock, er butchered, er swung up a gambrel-pin,
But what I thought o' John, and wished that he was home
  ag'in.

He'd come, sometimes—on Sund'ys most—and stay the
  Sund'y out;
And on Thanksgivin'-Day he 'peared to like to be about:
But a change was workin' on him—he was stiller than
  before,
And didn't joke, ner laugh, ner sing and whistle any more.

And his talk was all so proper; and I noticed, with a sigh,
He was tryin' to raise side-whiskers, and had on a striped
  tie,
And a standin'-collar, ironed up as stiff and slick as bone;
And a breast-pin, and a watch and chain and plug-hat of
  his own.

But when Spring-weather opened out, and John was to
  come home
And he'p me through the season, I was glad to see him
  come;
But my happiness, that evening, with the settin' sun went
  down,
When he bragged of "a position" that was offered him in
  town.

42

"But," says I, "you'll not accept it?" "W'y, of course I
         will," says he.—
"This drudgin' on a farm," he says, "is not the life fer
         me;
I've set my stakes up higher," he continued, light and gay,
"And town's the place fer *me*, and I'm a-goin' right
         away!"

And go he did!—his mother clingin' to him at the gate,
A-pleadin' and a-cryin'; but it hadn't any weight.
I was tranquiller, and told her 'twarn't no use to worry
         so,
And onclasped her arms from round his neck round mine
         —and let him go!

I felt a little bitter feelin' foolin' round about
The aidges of my conscience; but I didn't let it out;—
I simply retch out, trimbly-like, and tuk the boy's hand,
And though I didn't say a word, I knowed he'd under-
         stand.

And—well!—sence then the old home here was mighty
         lonesome, shore!
With me a-workin' in the field, and Mother at the door,

Her face ferever to'rds the town, and fadin' more and
        more—
Her only son nine miles away, a-clerkin' in a store!

The weeks and months dragged by us; and sometimes the
        boy would write
A letter to his mother, sayin' that his work was light,
And not to feel oneasy about his health a bit—
Though his business was confinin',' he was gittin' used
        to it.

And sometimes he would write and ast how *I* was gittin'
        on,
And ef I had to pay out much fer he'p sence he was gone;
And how the hogs was doin,' and the balance of the stock,
And talk on fer a page er two jest like he used to talk.

And he wrote, along 'fore harvest, that he guessed he
        would git home,
Fer business would, of course, be dull in town.—But
        didn't come:—
We got a postal later, sayin' when they had no trade
They filled the time "invoicin' goods," and that was why
        he stayed.

And then he quit a-writin' altogether: Not a word—
Exceptin' what the neighbors brung who'd been to town
     and heard
What store John was clerkin' in, and went round to in-
     quire
If they could buy their goods there less and sell their
     produce higher.

And so the Summer faded out, and Autumn wore away,
And a keener Winter never fetched around Thanksgivin'-
     Day!
The night before that day of thanks I'll never quite fergit,
The wind a-howlin' round the house—it makes me creepy
     yit!

And there set me and Mother—me a-twistin' at the prongs
Of a green scrub-ellum forestick with a vicious pair of
     tongs,
And Mother sayin,' *"David! David!"* in a' undertone,
As though she thought that I was thinkin' bad-words
     unbeknown.

"I've dressed the turkey, David, fer to-morrow," Mother
     said,
A-tryin' to wedge some pleasant subject in my stubborn
     head,—

49

"And the mince-meat I'm a-mixin' is perfection mighty
        nigh;
And the pound-cake is delicious-rich—" "Who'll eat
        'em?" I-says-I.

"The cramberries is drippin'-sweet," says Mother, runnin'
        on,
P'tendin' not to hear me;—"and somehow I thought of
        John
All the time they was a-jellin'—fer you know they allus
        was
His favo*rite*—he likes 'em so!" Says I, "Well, s'pose
        he does?"

"Oh, nothin' much!" says Mother, with a quiet sort o'
        smile—
"This gentleman behind my cheer may tell you after
        while!"
And as I turnt and looked around, some one riz up and
        leant
And putt his arms round Mother's neck, and laughed in
        low content.

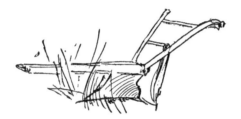

"It's *me*," he says—"your fool-boy John, come back to
    shake your hand;
Set down with you, and talk with you, and make you un-
    derstand
How dearer yit than all the world is this old home that
    we
Will spend Thanksgivin' in fer life—jest Mother, you
    and me!"

    .   .   .   .

Nobody on the old farm here but Mother, me and John,
Except, of course, the extry he'p, when harvest-time comes
    on;
And then, I want to say to you, we *need* sich he'p about,
As you'd admit, ef you could see the way the crops turns
    out!

53

A CANARY AT THE FARM

FOLKS has be'n to town, and Sahry
      Fetched 'er home a pet canary,—
And of all the blame', contrary,
      Aggervatin' things alive!
I love music—that's I love it
When it's *free*—and plenty of it;—
But I kindo' git above it,
      At a dollar-eighty-five!

Reason's plain as I'm a-sayin',—
Jes' the idy, now, o' layin'
Out yer money, and a-payin'
      Fer a willer-cage and bird,
When the medder-larks is wingin'
Round you, and the woods is ringin'
With the beautifullest singin'
      That a mortal ever heard!

Sahry's sot, tho.'—So I tell her
He's a purty little feller,
With his wings o' creamy-yeller,
      And his eyes keen as a cat;
And the twitter o' the critter
'Pears to absolutely glitter!
Guess I'll haf to go and git her
      A high-priceter cage 'n that!

WHERE THE CHILDREN USED TO PLAY

THE old farm-home is Mother's yet and mine,
    And filled it is with plenty and to spare,—
But we are lonely here in life's decline,
    Though fortune smiles around us everywhere:
        We look across the gold
        Of the harvests, as of old—
    The corn, the fragrant clover, and the hay;
        But most we turn our gaze,
        As with eyes of other days,
    To the orchard where the children used to play.

O from our life's full measure
And rich hoard of worldly treasure
    We often turn our weary eyes away,
And hand in hand we wander
Down the old path winding yonder
    To the orchard where the children used to play.

Our sloping pasture-lands are filled with herds;
    The barn and granary-bins are bulging o'er:
The grove's a paradise of singing birds—
    The woodland brook leaps laughing by the door;
            Yet lonely, lonely still,
            Let us prosper as we will,
    Our old hearts seem so empty everyway—
            We can only through a mist
            See the faces we have kissed
    In the orchard where the children used to play.

O from our life's full measure
And rich hoard of worldly treasure
    We often turn our weary eyes away,
And hand in hand we wander
Down the old path winding yonder
    To the orchard where the children used to play.

GRIGGSBY'S STATION

P AP'S got his pattent-right, and rich as all creation;
  But where's the peace and comfort that we all had
      before?
Le's go a-visitin' back to Griggsby's Station—
  Back where we ust to be so happy and so pore!

The likes of us a-livin' here! It's jest a mortal pity
  To see us in this great big house, with cyarpets on the
      stairs,
And the pump right in the kitchen! And the city! city!
      city!—
  And nothin' but the city all around us ever'wheres!

Climb clean above the roof and look from the steeple,
    And never see a robin, nor a beech or ellum tree!
And right here in ear-shot of at least a thousan' people,
    And none that neighbors with us or we want to go and
        see!

Le's go a-visitin' back to Griggsby's Station—
    Back where the latch-string's a-hangin' from the door,
And ever' neighbor round the place is dear as a relation—
    Back where we ust to be so happy and so pore!

I want to see the Wiggenses, the whole kit-and-bilin',
    A-drivin' up from Shallor Ford to stay the Sunday
        through;
And I want to see 'em hitchin' at their son-in-law's and
        pilin'
    Out there at 'Lizy Ellen's like they ust to do!

I want to see the piece-quilts the Jones girls is makin';
   And I want to pester Laury 'bout their freckled hired
        hand,
And joke her 'bout the widower she come purt' nigh a-
        takin',
   Till her Pap got his pension 'lowed in time to save his
        land.

Le's go a-visitin' back to Griggsby's Station—
   Back where they's nothin' aggervatin' any more,
Shet away safe in the woods around the old location—
   Back where we ust to be so happy and so pore!

I want to see Marindy and he'p her with her sewin',
   And hear her talk so lovin' of her man that's dead and
        gone,
And stand up with Emanuel to show me how he's
        growin',
   And smile as I have saw her 'fore she putt her mournin'
        on.

And I want to see the Samples, on the old lower eighty,
    Where John, our oldest boy, he was tuk and burried
           —for
His own sake and Katy's,—and I want to cry with Katy
    As she reads all his letters over, writ from The War.

What's in all this grand life and high situation,
    And nary pink nor hollyhawk a-bloomin' at the door?—
Le's go a-visitin' back to Griggsby's Station—
    Back where we ust to be so happy and so pore!

KNEE-DEEP IN JUNE

I

TELL you what I like the best—
　　'Long about knee-deep in June,
　　'Bout the time strawberries melts
　　On the vine,—some afternoon
Like to jes' git out and rest,
　　And not work at nothin' else!

II

Orchard's where I'd ruther be—
Needn't fence it in fer me!—
    Jes' the whole sky overhead,
And the whole airth underneath—
Sort o' so's a man kin breathe
    Like he ort, and kind o' has
Elbow-room to keerlessly
        Sprawl out len'thways on the grass
            Where the shadders thick and soft
        As the kivvers on the bed
            Mother fixes in the loft
Allus, when they's company!

III

Jes' a-sorto' lazin there—
    S'lazy, 'at you peek and peer
        Through the wavin' leaves above,
        Like a feller 'at's in love
    And don't know it, ner don't keer!
    Ever'thing you hear and see
        Got some sort o' interest—
        Maybe find a bluebird's nest

Tucked up there conveenently
Fer the boy 'at's ap' to be
Up some other apple-tree!
Watch the swallers skootin' past
'Bout as peert as you could ast;
 Er the Bob-white raise and whiz
 Where some other's whistle is.

IV

Ketch a shadder down below,
And look up to find the crow—
Er a hawk,—away up there,
'Pearantly *froze* in the air!—
 Hear the old hen squawk, and squat
 Over ever' chick she's got,
  Suddent-like!—and she knows where
 That-air hawk is, well as you!—
 You jes' bet yer life she do!—
  Eyes a-glitterin' like glass,
  Waitin' till he makes a pass!

V

Pee-wees' singin', to express
 My opinion, 's second class,

Yit you'll hear 'em more er less;
　　Sapsucks gittin' down to biz,
Weedin' out the lonesomeness;
　　Mr. Bluejay, full o' sass,
　　In them base-ball clothes o' his,
Sportin' round the orchard jes'
Like he owned the premises!
　　Sun out in the fields kin sizz,
But flat on yer back, I guess,
　　In the shade's where glory is!
That's jes' what I'd like to do
Stiddy fer a year er two!

VI

Plague! ef they ain't somepin' in
Work 'at kindo' goes ag'in'
　　My convictions!—'long about
　　　Here in June especially!—
　　　Under some old apple-tree,
　　　　Jes' a-restin through and through,
　　I could git along without
　　　　Nothin' else at all to do
　　　　Only jes' a-wishin' you

Wuz a-gittin' there like me,
And June was eternity!

VII

Lay out there and try to see
Jes' how lazy you kin be!—
      Tumble round and souse yer head
In the clover-bloom, er pull
          Yer straw hat acrost yer eyes
          And peek through it at the skies,
       Thinkin' of old chums 'at's dead,
             Maybe, smilin' back at you
In betwixt the beautiful
          Clouds o' gold and white and blue!—
Month a man kin railly love—
June, you know, I'm talkin' of!

VIII

March ain't never nothin' new!—
April's altogether too
    Brash fer me! and May—I jes'
    'Bominate its promises,—
Little hints o' sunshine and
Green around the timber-land—

A few blossoms, and a few
Chip-birds, and a sprout er two,—
Drap asleep, and it turns in
'Fore daylight and *snows* ag'in!—
But when *June* comes—Clear my th'oat
With wild honey!—Rench my hair
In the dew! And hold my coat!
Whoop out loud! And th'ow my hat!—
June wants me, and I'm to spare!
Spread them shadders anywhere,
I'll get down and waller there,
And obleeged to you at that!

SEPTEMBER DARK

I

THE air falls chill;
  The whippoorwill
Pipes lonesomely behind the hill:
The dusk grows dense,
The silence tense;
And lo, the katydids commence.

79

II

Through shadowy rifts
Of woodland, lifts
The low, slow moon, and upward drifts,
While left and right
The fireflies' light
Swirls eddying in the skirts of Night.

III

O Cloudland, gray
And level, lay
Thy mists across the face of Day!
At foot and head,
Above the dead,
O Dews, weep on uncomforted!

THE CLOVER

SOME sings of the lily, and daisy, and rose,
　　And the pansies and pinks that the Summertime
　　　　throws
In the green grassy lap of the medder that lays
Blinkin' up at the skyes through the sunshiney days;
But what is the lily and all of the rest
Of the flowers, to a man with a hart in his brest
That was dipped brimmin' full of the honey and dew
Of the sweet clover-blossoms his babyhood knew?

THE CLOVER

I never set eyes on a clover-field now,
Er fool round a stable, er climb in the mow,
But my childhood comes back jest as clear and as plane
As the smell of the clover I'm sniffin' again;
And I wunder away in a bare-footed dream,
Whare I tangle my toes in the blossoms that gleam
With the dew of the dawn of the morning of love
Ere it wept ore the graves that I'm weepin' above.

And so I love clover—it seems like a part
Of the sacerdest sorrows and joys of my hart;
And wharever it blossoms, oh, thare let me bow
And thank the good God as I'm thankin' Him now;
And I pray to Him still fer the stren'th when I die,
To go out in the clover and tell it good-bye,
And lovin'ly nestle my face in its bloom
While my soul slips away on a breth of purfume.

OLD OCTOBER

OLD October's purt' nigh gone,
And the frosts is comin' on
Little *heavier* every day—
Like our hearts is thataway!
Leaves is changin' overhead
Back from green to gray and red,
Brown and yeller, with their stems
Loosenin' on the oaks and e'ms;
And the balance of the trees
Gittin' balder every breeze—
Like the heads we're scratchin' on!
Old October's purt' nigh gone.

I love Old October so,
I can't bear to see her go—
Seems to me like losin' some
Old-home relative er chum—
'Pears like sorto' settin' by
Some old friend 'at sigh by sigh
Was a-passin' out o' sight
Into everlastin' night!
Hickernuts a feller hears
Rattlin' down is more like tears
Drappin' on the leaves below—
I love Old October so!

Can't tell what it is about
Old October knocks me out!—
I sleep well enough at night—
And the blamedest appetite
Ever mortal man possessed,—
Last thing et, it tastes the best!—
Warnuts, butternuts, pawpaws,
'Iles and limbers up my jaws
Fer raal service, sich as new
Pork, spareribs, and sausage, too.—
Yit, fer all, they's somepin' 'bout
Old October knocks me out!

OLD-FASHIONED ROSES

THEY ain't no style about 'em,
    And they're sorto' pale and faded,
Yit the doorway here, without 'em,
    Would be lonesomer, and shaded
        With a good 'eal blacker shadder
            Than the morning-glories makes,
        And the sunshine would look sadder
            Fer their good old-fashion' sakes.

I like 'em 'cause they kindo'-
    Sorto' *make* a feller like 'em!
And I tell you, when I find a
    Bunch out whur the sun kin strike 'em,

It allus sets me thinkin'
    O' the ones 'at used to grow
And peek in thro' the chinkin'
    O' the cabin, don't you know!

And then I think o' mother,
    And how she ust to love 'em—
When they wuzn't any other,
    'Less she found 'em up above 'em!
        And her eyes, afore she shut 'em,
            Whispered with a smile and said
        We must pick a bunch and putt 'em
            In her hand when she wuz dead.

But, as I wuz a-sayin',
    They ain't no style about 'em
Very gaudy er displayin',
    But I wouldn't be without 'em,—
        'Cause I'm happier in these posies,
            And the hollyhawks and sich,
        Than the hummin'-bird 'at noses
            In the roses of the rich.

A COUNTRY PATHWAY

I COME upon it suddenly, alone—
    A little pathway winding in the weeds
That fringe the roadside; and with dreams my own,
   I wander as it leads.

Full wistfully along the slender way,
   Through summer tan of freckled shade and shine,
I take the path that leads me as it may—
   Its every choice is mine.

A chipmunk, or a sudden-whirring quail,
    Is startled by my step as on I fare—
A garter-snake across the dusty trail
    Glances and—is not there.

Above the arching jimson-weeds flare twos
    And twos of sallow-yellow butterflies,
Like blooms of lorn primroses blowing loose
    When autumn winds arise.

The trail dips—dwindles—broadens then, and lifts
    Itself astride a cross-road dubiously,
And, from the fennel marge beyond it, drifts
    Still onward, beckoning me.

And though it needs must lure me mile on mile
    Out of the public highway, still I go,
My thoughts, far in advance in Indian-file,
    Allure me even so.

Why, I am as a long-lost boy that went
    At dusk to bring the cattle to the bars,
And was not found again, though Heaven lent
    His mother all the stars

With which to seek him through that awful night.
 O years of nights as vain!—Stars never rise
But well might miss their glitter in the light
 Of tears in mother-eyes!

So—on, with quickened breaths, I follow still—
 My avant-courier must be obeyed!
Thus am I led, and thus the path, at will,
 Invites me to invade

A meadow's precincts, where my daring guide
 Clambers the steps of an old-fashioned stile,
And stumbles down again, the other side,
 To gambol there awhile.

In pranks of hide-and-seek, as on ahead
 I see it running, while the clover-stalks
Shake rosy fists at me, as though they said—
 "You dog our country-walks

"And mutilate us with your walking-stick!—
 We will not suffer tamely what you do,
And warn you at your peril,—for we'll sic
 Our bumblebees on you!"

But I smile back, in airy nonchalance,—
    The more determined on my wayward quest,
As some bright memory a moment dawns
    A morning in my breast—

Sending a thrill that hurries me along
    In faulty similes of childish skips,
Enthused with lithe contortions of a song
    Performing on my lips.

In wild meanderings o'er pasture wealth—
    Erratic wanderings through dead'ning-lands,
Where sly old brambles, plucking me by stealth,
    Put berries in my hands:

Or the path climbs a bowlder—wades a slough—
    Or, rollicking through buttercups and flags,
Goes gayly dancing o'er a deep bayou
    On old tree-trunks and snags:

Or, at the creek, leads o'er a limpid pool
    Upon a bridge the stream itself has made,
With some Spring-freshet for the mighty tool
    That its foundation laid.

I pause a moment here to bend and muse,
    With dreamy eyes, on my reflection, where
A boat-backed bug drifts on a helpless cruise,
    Or wildly oars the air,

As, dimly seen, the pirate of the brook—
    The pike, whose jaunty hulk denotes his speed—
Swings pivoting about, with wary look
    Of low and cunning greed.

Till, filled with other thought, I turn again
    To where the pathway enters in a realm
Of lordly woodland, under sovereign reign
    Of towering oak and elm.

A puritanic quiet here reviles
    The almost whispered warble from the hedge,
And takes a locust's rasping voice and files
    The silence to an edge.

In such a solitude my somber way
    Strays like a misanthrope within a gloom
Of his own shadows—till the perfect day
    Bursts into sudden bloom,

And crowns a long, declining stretch of space,
　　Where King Corn's armies lie with flags unfurled,
And where the valley's dint in Nature's face
　　Dimples a smiling world.

And lo! through mists that may not be dispelled,
　　I see an old farm homestead, as in dreams,
Where, like a gem in costly setting held,
　　The old log cabin gleams.

　　　　．　．　．　．　．　．　．　．　．

O darling Pathway! lead me bravely on
　　Adown your valley-way, and run before
Among the roses crowding up the lawn
　　And thronging at the door,—

And carry up the echo there that shall
　　Arouse the drowsy dog, that he may bay
The household out to greet the prodigal
　　That wanders home to-day.

WORTERMELON TIME

OLD wortermelon time is a-comin' round again,
 And they ain't no man a-livin' any tickleder'n me,
Fer the way I hanker after wortermelons is a sin—
 Which is the why and wharefore, as you can plainly see.

Oh! it's in the sandy soil wortermelons does the best,
 And it's thare they'll lay and waller in the sunshine and
   the dew
Tel they wear all the green streaks clean off of theyr
   breast;
 And you bet I ain't a-findin' any fault with them; air
   you?

They ain't no better thing in the vegetable line;
    And they don't need much 'tendin', as ev'ry farmer
        knows;
And when theyr ripe and ready fer to pluck from the vine,
    I want to say to you theyr the best fruit that grows.

It's some likes the yeller-core, and some likes the red,
    And it's some says "The Little Californy" is the best;
But the sweetest slice of all I ever wedged in my head,
    Is the old "Edingburg Mounting-sprout," of the west.

You don't want no punkins nigh your wortermelon vines—
    'Cause, some-way-another, they'll spile your melons,
        shore;—
I've seed 'em taste like punkins, from the core to the rines,
    Which may be a fact you have heerd of before.

But your melons that's raised right and 'tended to with
        care,
    You can walk around amongst 'em with a parent's pride
        and joy,
And thump 'em on the heads with as fatherly a air
    As ef each one of them was your little girl er boy.

I joy in my hart jest to hear that rippin' sound
    When you split one down the back and jolt the halves in
        two,
And the friends you love the best is gethered all around—
    And you says unto your sweethart, "Oh, here's the core
        fer you!"

And I like to slice 'em up in big pieces fer 'em all,
    Espeshally the childern, and watch theyr high delight
As one by one the rines with theyr pink notches falls,
    And they holler fer some more, with unquenched
        appetite.

Boys takes to it natchurl, and I like to see 'em eat—
    A slice of wortermelon's like a frenchharp in theyr
        hands,
And when they "saw" it through theyr mouth sich music
        can't be beat—
    'Cause it's music both the sperit and the stummick
        understands.

Oh, they's more in wortermelons than the purty-colored
        meat,
    And the overflowin' sweetness of the worter squshed
        betwixt

The up'ard and the down'ard motions of a feller's teeth,
   And it's the taste of ripe old age and juicy childhood
      mixed.

Fer I never taste a melon but my thoughts flies away
   To the summertime of youth; and again I see the dawn,
And the fadin' afternoon of the long summer day,
   And the dusk and dew a-fallin', and the night a-comin'
      on.

And thare's the corn around us, and the lispin' leaves and
      trees,
   And the stars a-peekin' down on us as still as silver
      mice,
And us boys in the wortermelons on our hands and knees,
   And the new-moon hangin' ore us like a yeller-cored
      slice.

Oh! it's wortermelon time is a-comin' round again,
   And they ain't no man a-livin' any tickleder'n me,
Fer the way I hanker after wortermelons is a sin—
   Which is the why and wharefore, as you can plainly see.

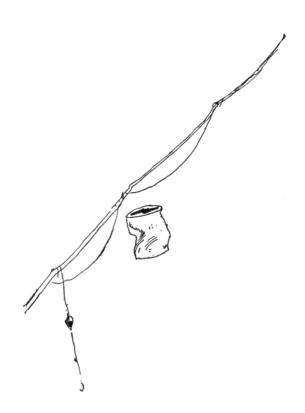

UP AND DOWN OLD BRANDYWINE

UP and down old Brandywine,
    In the days 'at's past and gone—
With a dad-burn hook-and-line
    And a saplin'-pole—i swawn!
        I've had more fun, to the square
        Inch, than ever *any*where!
        Heaven to come can't discount *mine*
        Up and down old Brandywine!

113

Hain't no sense in *wishin'*—yit
    Wisht to goodness I *could* jes
"Gee" the blame' world round and git
    Back to that old happiness!—
        Kindo' drive back in the shade
         "The old Covered Bridge" there laid
        'Crosst the crick, and sorto' soak
        My soul over, hub and spoke!

Honest, now!—it hain't no *dream*
    'At I'm wantin',—but *the fac's*
As they wuz; the same old stream,
    And the same old times, i jacks!—
        Gim me back my bare feet—and
        Stonebruise too!—and scratched and tanned!
        And let hottest dog-days shine
        Up and down old Brandywine!

In and on betwixt the trees
    'Long the banks, pour down yer noon,
Kindo' curdled with the breeze
    And the yallerhammer's tune;

And the smokin', chokin' dust
O' the turnpike at its wusst—
Saturd'ys, say, when it seems
Road's jes jammed with country teams!—

Whilse the old town, fur away
    'Crosst the hazy pastur'-land,
Dozed-like in the heat o' day
    Peaceful' as a hired hand.
        Jolt the gravel th'ough the floor
        O' the old bridge!—grind and roar
        With yer blame percession-line—
        Up and down old Brandywine!

Souse me and my new straw-hat
    Off the foot-log!—what *I* care?—
Fist shoved in the crown o' that—
    Like the old Clown ust to wear.
        Wouldn't swop it fer a' old
        Gin-u-wine raal crown o' gold!—
        Keep yer *King* ef you'll gim me
        Jes the boy I ust to be!

Spill my fishin'-worms! er steal
　　My best "goggle-eye!"—but you
Can't lay hands on joys I feel
　　Nibblin' like they ust to do!
　　　　So, in memory, to-day
　　　　Same old ripple lips away
　　　　At my "cork" and saggin' line,
　　　　Up and down old Bradywine!

There the logs is, round the hill,
　　Where "Old Irvin" ust to lift
Out sunfish from daylight till
　　Dewfall—'fore he'd leave "The Drift"
　　　　And give *us* a chance—and then
　　　　Kindo' fish back home again,
　　　　Ketchin' 'em jes left and right
　　　　Where we hadn't got "a bite!"

Er, 'way windin' out and in,—
　　Old path th'ough the iurnweeds
And dog-fennel to yer chin—
　　Then come suddent, th'ough the reeds

And cat-tails, smack into where
Them-air woods-hogs ust to scare
Us clean 'crosst the County-line,
Up and down old Brandywine!

But the dim roar o' the dam
   It 'ud coax us furder still
To'rds the old race, slow and ca'm,
   Slidin' on to Huston's mill—
      Where, I 'spect, "The Freeport crowd"
      Never *warmed* to us er 'lowed
      We wuz quite so overly
      Welcome as we aimed to be.

Still it 'peared like ever'thing—
   Fur away from home as *there*—
Had more *relish*-like, i jing!—
   Fish in stream, er bird in air!
      O them rich old bottom-lands,
      Past where Cowden's Schoolhouse stands!
      Wortermelons—*master-mine!*
      Up and down old Brandywine!

And sich pop-paws!—Lumps o' raw
    Gold and green,—jes oozy th'ough
With ripe yaller—like you've saw
    Custard-pie with no crust to:
        And jes *gorges* o' wild plums,
        Till a feller'd suck his thumbs
        Clean up to his elbows! *My!*—
        Me some more er lem me die!

Up and down old Brandywine! . . .
    Stripe me with pokeberry-juice!—
Flick me with a pizenvine
    And yell *"Yip!"* and lem me loose!
        —Old now as I then wuz young,
        'F I could sing as I *have* sung,
        Song 'ud surely ring *dee-vine*
        Up and down old Brandywine!

WHEN EARLY MARCH SEEMS MIDDLE
MAY

WHEN country roads begin to thaw
  In mottled spots of damp and dust,
And fences by the margin draw
    Along the frosty crust
    Their graphic silhouettes, I say,
    The Spring is coming round this way.

When morning-time is bright with sun
   And keen with wind, and both confuse
The dancing, glancing eyes of one
      With tears that ooze and ooze—
   And nose-tips weep as well as they,
   The Spring is coming round this way.

When suddenly some shadow-bird
   Goes wavering beneath the gaze,
And through the hedge the moan is heard
      Of kine that fain would graze
   In grasses new, I smile and say,
   The Spring is coming round this way.

When knotted horse-tails are untied,
   And teamsters whistle here and there.
And clumsy mitts are laid aside
      And choppers' hands are bare,
   And chips are thick where children play,
   The Spring is coming round this way.

When through the twigs the farmer tramps,
   And troughs are chunked beneath the trees,
And fragrant hints of sugar-camps
      Astray in every breeze,—

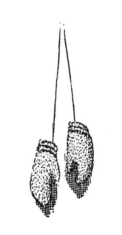

When early March seems middle May,
The Spring is coming round this way.

When coughs are changed to laughs, and when
    Our frowns melt into smiles of glee,
And all our blood thaws out again
        In streams of ecstasy,
    And poets wreak their roundelay,
    The Spring is coming round this way.

A TALE
OF THE
AIRLY DAYS

OH! tell me a tale of the airly days—
　　Of the times as they ust to be;
"Piller of Fi-er" and "Shakespeare's Plays"
　　Is a' most too deep fer me!
I want plane facts, and I want plane words,
　　Of the good old-fashioned ways,
When speech run free as the songs of birds
　　'Way back in the airly days.

Tell me a tale of the timber-lands—
    Of the old-time pioneers;
Somepin' a pore man understands
    With his feelins 's well as ears.
Tell of the old log house,—about
    The loft, and the puncheon flore—
The old fi-er-place, with the crane swung out,
    And the latch-string thrugh the door.

Tell of the things jest as they was—
    They don't need no excuse!—
Don't tech 'em up like the poets does,
    Tel theyr all too fine fer use!—
Say they was 'leven in the fambily—
    Two beds, and the chist, below,
And the trundle-beds that each helt three,
    And the clock and the old bureau.

Then blow the horn at the old back-door
    Tel the echoes all halloo,
And the childern gethers home onc't more,
    Jest as they ust to do:

Blow fer Pap tel he hears and comes,
　　With Tomps and Elias, too,
A-marchin' home, with the fife and drums
　　And the old Red White and Blue!

Blow and blow tel the sound draps low
　　As the moan of the whipperwill,
And wake up Mother, and Ruth and Jo,
　　All sleepin' at Bethel Hill:
Blow and call tel the faces all
　　Shine out in the back-log's blaze,
And the shadders dance on the old hewed wall
　　As they did in the airly days.

OLD MAN'S NURSERY RHYME

I

IN the jolly winters
  Of the long-ago,
It was not so cold as now—
  O! No! No!
Then, as I remember,
  Snowballs to eat
Were as good as apples now.
  And every bit as sweet!

II

In the jolly winters
     Of the dead-and-gone,
Bub was warm as summer,
     With his red mitts on,—
Just in his little waist-
     And-pants all together,
Who ever hear him growl
     About cold weather?

III

In the jolly winters
     Of the long-ago—
Was it *half* so cold as now?
     O! No! No!
Who caught his death o' cold,
     Making prints of men
Flat-backed in snow that now's
     Twice as cold again?

IV

In the jolly winters
 Of the dead-and-gone,
Startin' out rabbit-huntin'—
 Early as the dawn,—
Who ever froze his fingers,
 Ears, heels, or toes,—
Or'd 'a' cared if he had?
 Nobody knows!

V

Nights by the kitchen-stove,
 Shellin' white and red
Corn in the skillet, and
 Sleepin' four abed!
Ah! the jolly winters
 Of the long-ago!
We were not as old as now—
 O! No! No!

JUNE

O QUEENLY month of indolent repose!
    I drink thy breath in sips of rare perfume,
As in thy downy lap of clover-bloom
I nestle like a drowsy child and doze
The lazy hours away. The zephyr throws
    The shifting shuttle of the Summer's loom
    And weaves a damask-work of gleam and gloom
Before thy listless feet. The lily blows
    A bugle-call of fragrance o'er the glade;
        And, wheeling into ranks, with plume and spear,
    Thy harvest-armies gather on parade;
        While, faint and far away, yet pure and clear,
    A voice calls out of alien lands of shade:—
        All hail the Peerless Goddess of the Year!

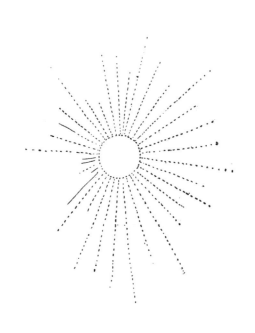

THE TREE-TOAD

"'S CUR'OUS-LIKE," said the tree-toad,
    "I've twittered fer rain all day;
   And I got up soon,
   And I hollered tel noon—
  But the sun, hit blazed away,
    Tell I jest clumb down in a crawfish-hole,
    Weary at hart, and sick at soul!

"Dozed away fer an hour,
　　And I tackled the thing agin:
　　　　And I sung, and sung,
　　　　Tel I knowed my lung
　　Was jest about give in;
　　　　And *then,* thinks I, ef hit don't rain *now,*
　　　　They's nothin' in singin,' anyhow!

"Onc't in a while some farmer
　　Would come a-drivin' past;
　　　　And he'd hear my cry,
　　　　And stop and sigh—
　　Tel I jest laid back, at last,
　　　　And I hollered rain tel I thought my th'oat
　　　　Would bust right open at ever' note!

"But I *fetched* her!—O *I fetched* her!—
　　'Cause a little while ago,
　　　　As I kindo' set,
　　　　With one eye shet,
　　And a-singin' soft and low,
　　　　A voice drapped down on my fevered brain,
　　　　A-sayin',—'Ef *you'll jest hush I'll rain!*'"

A SONG OF LONG AGO

A SONG of Long Ago:
    Sing it lightly—sing it low—
Sing it softly—like the lisping of the lips we
    used to know
When our baby-laughter spilled
From the glad hearts ever filled
With music blithe as robin ever trilled!

Let the fragrant summer breeze,
And the leaves of locust-trees,
And the apple-buds and blossoms, and the
      wings of honey-bees,
All palpitate with glee,
Till the happy harmony
Brings back each childish joy to you and me.

Let the eyes of fancy turn
Where the tumbled pippins burn
Like embers in the orchard's lap of tangled
      grass and fern,—
There let the old path wind
In and out and on behind
The cider-press that chuckles as we grind.

Blend in the song the moan
Of the dove that grieves alone,
And the wild whir of the locust, and the
      bumble's drowsy drone;
And the low of cows that call
Through the pasture-bars when all
The landscape fades away at evenfall.

Then, far away and clear,
Through the dusky atmosphere,
Let the wailing of the killdee be the only
      sound we hear:
O sad and sweet and low
As the memory may know
Is the glad-pathetic song of Long Ago!

OLD WINTERS ON THE FARM

I HAVE jest about decided
   It 'ud keep a *town-boy* hoppin'
   Fer to work all winter, choppin'
Fer a' old fire-place, like *I* did!
Lawz! them old times wuz contrairy!—
   Blame' backbone o' winter, 'peared-like,
   Wouldn't break!—and I wuz skeerd-like
Clean on into *Feb'uary!*
   Nothin' ever made me madder
Than fer Pap to stomp in, layin'
In a' extra forestick, sayin',
   "Groun'-hog's out and seed his shadder!"

ROMANCIN'

I' B'EN a-kindo *"musin',"* as the feller says, and I'm
   About o' the conclusion that they hain't no better
      time,
When you come to cipher on it, than the times we ust
   to know
When we swore our first *"dog-gone-it"* sorto' solum-like
   and low!

You git my idy, do you?—*Little* tads, you understand—
Jest a-wishin' thue and thue you that you on'y wuz a
    man.—
Yit here I am, this minit, even sixty, to a day,
And fergittin' all that's in it, wishin' jest the other way!

I hain't no hand to lectur' on the times, er *dim*onstrate
Whare the trouble is, er hector and domineer with Fate,—
But when I git so flurried, and so pestered-like and blue,
And so rail owdacious worried, let me tell you what I
    do!—

I jest gee-haw the hosses, and onhook the swingle-tree,
Whare the hazel-bushes tosses down theyr shadders over
    me;
And I draw my plug o' navy, and I climb the fence, and
    set
Jest a-thinkin' here, i gravy! tel my eyes is wringin'-wet!

Tho' I still kin see the trouble o' the *presunt,* I kin see—
Kindo' like my sight wuz double—all the things that
    ust to be;
And the flutter o' the robin and the teeter o' the wren
Sets the willer-branches bobbin' "howdy-do" thum *Now*
    to *Then!*

The deadnin' and the thicket's jest a-bilin' full of June,
From the rattle o' the cricket, to the yallar-hammer's
      tune;
And the catbird in the bottom, and the sapsuck on the
      snag,
Seems ef they can't—od-rot 'em!—jest do nothin' else
      but brag!

They's music in the twitter of the bluebird and the jay,
And that sassy little critter jest a-*peckin'* all the day;
They's music in the "flicker," and they's music in the
      thrush,
And they's music in the snicker o' the chipmunk in the
      brush!

They's music *all around* me!—and I go back, in a dream
Sweeter yit than ever found me fast asleep,—and in the
      stream
That ust to split the medder whare the dandylions
      growed,
I stand knee-deep, and redder than the sunset down the
      road.

Then's when I' b'en a-fishin'!—and they's other fellers,
      too,
With their hick'ry-poles a-swishin' out behind 'em; and
      a few
Little "shiners" on our stringers, with theyr tails tip-
      toein' bloom,
As we dance 'em in our fingers all the happy jurney
      home.

I kin see us, true to Natur', thum the time we started out,
With a biscuit and a 'tater in our little "roundabout"!—
I kin see our lines a-tanglin', and our elbows in a jam,
And our naked legs a-danglin' thum the apern o' the dam.

I kin see the honeysuckle climbin' up around the mill,
And kin hear the worter chuckle, and the wheel a-growl-
      in' still;
And thum the bank below it I kin steal the old canoe,
And jest git in and row it like the miller ust to do.

W'y, I git my fancy focussed on the past so mortul plane
I kin even smell the locus'-blossoms bloomin' in the lane;
And I hear the cow-bells clinkin' sweeter tunes 'n
      "Money-musk"
Fer the lightnin' bugs a-blinkin' and a-dancin' in the dusk.

And when I've kep' on "musin'," as the feller says, tel I'm
Firm-fixed in the conclusion that they hain't no better
  time,
When you come to cipher on it, than the *old* times,—I
  de-clare
I kin wake and say "dog-gone-it!" jest as soft as any
  prayer!

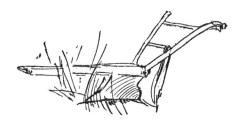

The first edition of this book, published by the Bobbs-Merrill Company of Indianapolis, was printed by the letterpress process in 1883 in a two-color (red and black) format, using either stereotype or electrotype plates made from the original linotype and foundry setting. The book was subsequently reprinted from these same plates in 1887, 1888, 1890, 1892, 1894, 1896, 1898, 1899, and 1905. Each printing caused a bit more wear on those printing plates, resulting in some smashed and worn letter shapes on many of the pages. The wash-drawing halftones, done in the copper-plated engraving process, survived better than the type.

For the 2013 edition, all the text has been reset using computer software, giving the poems new life while preserving as far as possible the feeling of the 1905 edition. Great care was taken by Sheridan Books, Inc. to scan the halftones and line drawings. The book was composed at Indiana University Press and printed by Sheridan Books, Inc. The text face is Arno, designed by Robert Slimbach in 2007, issued by Adobe Systems, Inc.